Living with questions
exploring faith and doubt

NICK FAWCETT

**kevin
mayhew**

First published in 2002 by
KEVIN MAYHEW LTD
Buxhall, Stowmarket, Suffolk IP14 3BW
Email: info@kevinmayhewltd.com

9 8 7 6 5 4 3 2 1 0

ISBN 1 84003 915 9
Catalogue No 1500507

Cover design by Angela Selfe
Edited by Katherine Laidler
Typesetting by Louise Selfe

Printed and bound in Great Britain

Living with questions
exploring faith and doubt

Contents

To Alice Woodfine
in loving memory of Albert,
with many fond and thankful
recollections of you both

Acknowledgements

Bible quotations are taken from the New Revised Standard Version of the Bible, copyright © 1989 by the Division of Christian Education of the National Council of the Churches of Christ in the USA. Used by permission. All rights reserved.

Introduction

When I was at college, training for the ministry, I experienced a time of deep and disturbing doubt. So severe was this that there were times when I wondered whether I believed anything or whether I'd lost my faith completely. I'd always thought I was open-minded, but my studies in theology, philosophy, comparative religion and much else opened my eyes to a host of questions that I'd never seriously considered before, forcing me to realise that everything was not as straightforward as I'd previously liked to imagine. Eventually, in some despair, I knocked on the college principal's door and asked if I could talk things through. To my surprise, he seemed relieved rather than shocked at my doubt, glad that I was less certain than I'd once been. 'It's those who don't come to me, I worry about,' he confided. 'Those who question are ready to learn.'

I never forgot that interview, for it was a turning point in my life. Until then, I'd felt guilty, ashamed to admit there were things I wasn't sure of, worried that I was letting not just myself down but God as well, not to mention those in my home church who'd supported my call to ministry. Suddenly here was a new perspective, a voice assuring me that I was there in the wilderness for a purpose and that my questions were part of my pilgrimage of faith. It was a long hard road, and there were times when I longed for the comfortable security afforded by unquestioning dogma and revealed certainties, but, looking back, I realise that faith was tested, shaped and enriched through being stretched. Certainly it emerged different from before – less narrow, less assertive, less self-assured – but it was also stronger for what it had been through – more able to take whatever life might throw at it and still stand firm.

All this is not to say that every question is good. Sometimes, we can ask the wrong things at the wrong times in the wrong way for the wrong reasons, our questions serving only to damage and destroy, and doubt ultimately proving a significant step towards disbelief. Nor would I pretend that every mystery can be resolved, any more than I would claim to have all the answers. Questions can be good or bad, right or wrong, and it is a fine line between the two. Earnest seeking is not the same thing as cynical scepticism. How far an enquiring mind is an asset and how far a danger, is perhaps the most important question of all, and it does not admit to simplistic solutions.

This book, then, aims to take a balanced look at faith and doubt. It is written out of the conviction that there are many Christians troubled by uncertainties which they feel uneasy about voicing, and many outside the Church who feel that their honest misgivings concerning religion preclude them from considering the challenge of the gospel. If I am wrong, no one will buy this book and writing it will prove to have been a waste of time, but if I am right, I hope some at least may come to recognise that their questions can be a sign of strength rather than weakness, of faith rather than doubt; each an integral step in an unfolding journey of discipleship.

Nick Fawcett

Leader's notes

I suggest using the material in this book as follows:

- Each session begins with a traditional prayer, followed by a short paragraph introducing the overall theme. It is worth reading this aloud, to set the scene for the session.

- After this I have included 'Activity' sessions, designed to break the ice and to encourage informal reflection on the theme of the study. Allow ten minutes or so for these, but do not allow them to dominate the session.

- Next comes a Bible passage (my own paraphrase unless otherwise stated). This should be read aloud, and then time given for group members to quietly ponder its meaning.

- Ideally, group members need to have read the 'Comment' section before the meeting, in which case you will need to have circulated booklets in advance of the first session. Alternatively, extend the period of quiet after the reading so that participants can read this section at their own pace.

- The 'Summary' section highlights the key points of the Comment. The leader should read this aloud before inviting people's thoughts on the subject so far.

- Allow discussion to develop, and introduce as appropriate the questions provided in the Discussion section. It may be appropriate at this point to bring in the passage suggested for further reading, though you may prefer to leave this, as I have done, to round off the theme nearer the end.

- Pause for prayer, using the prayer provided, a prayer of your own, or a time of quiet/open prayer.

- After allowing ample time for discussion, read the meditation to draw people's thoughts together. The meditation in week 3 was written specially for this book; the others are taken from my earlier publications *No Ordinary Man, Are You Listening?* and *Grappling with God*.

- Briefly outline the suggestions for action. Invite any further ideas from among the group. From the second week onwards, you might also give people the opportunity to share how they applied the suggestions from the previous week.
- Finally, end the meeting in prayer, using either the prayer provided or your own.

Prayer

Eternal God,
    there are so many things we are uncertain about,
    so many complicated and confusing areas of life.
Grant us faith to live with questions
    and wisdom in coming to decisions.
Lord, we believe;
    help our unbelief.

We know you are at work in the world,
    and we believe in the final victory of your purpose,
    yet it is hard sometimes to see your hand
    and harder still to make sense of the events that befall us.
We see much that challenges and even seems to contradict our faith,
    and at times, despite ourselves, our trust is undermined
    and our confidence shaken.
Give us help to hold on to you,
    knowing that you hold on to us.
Lord, we believe;
    help our unbelief.

Teach us that doubts and questions are a part of faith,
    able to lead us to new insights
    and a deeper understanding of your purpose.
Give us the courage we need to be honest with you
    and with ourselves,
    open to that which stretches and challenges
    our comfortable preconceptions.
Help us to recognise that before building
    there must sometimes be demolition,
    before growth, a time of pruning,
    before receiving, a time of letting go.
Lord, we believe;
    help our unbelief.

Teach us the limitations of questions,
    the boundaries of our understanding,
        and so help us to know when it is right to ask
        and important to listen,
        necessary to seek further or time to live with mystery.
Lord, we believe;
    help our unbelief.

Teach us, then, to bring both our faith and doubt to you,
    confident that you can use both
    to broaden our knowledge of your love
    and to enrich our experience of your grace.
Lord, we believe;
    help our unbelief.
In Jesus' name we ask it.
Amen.

First week

Learning through questions

Opening prayer

O Lord my God,
  teach my heart this day
  where and how to see you,
  where and how to find you.
You have made and remade me,
  and you have given to me
  all the truly good things I possess,
  and still I do not know you.
I have not yet done that for which I was created.
Teach me to seek you,
  for I cannot seek you unless you teach me,
  or find you unless you show yourself to me.
Let me seek you in my longing,
  let me long for you in my seeking.
Let me find you by loving you,
  let me love you when I find you.
Amen.

St Anselm

Introduction

A while back, I was lucky enough to attend a recording of the long-running radio series *Gardeners' Question Time*. I'd often heard snippets of the programme before that, but sitting in the audience as the panellists responded off the cuff to an astonishingly broad selection of questions brought home to me the breadth of their expertise and the paucity of my own gardening knowledge by comparison. That is not to say I cannot learn more. Indeed, the chief reason for the popularity of the programme, at the time of writing in its fifty-fifth year, is that it makes use of one of the most effective learning tools there is: asking questions and listening to the answers. Across the country, people regularly tune in because they want to find out more and so fill in the gaps in their knowledge.

Sadly, when it comes to faith Christians are sometimes reluctant to ask questions. With some, this reflects apathy and disinterest, the original spark of faith all but extinguished, with little interest in rekindling it. For others, it is more a question of complacency, a naïve assumption that faith will grow by itself with no effort on our part, that God will somehow spoon-feed us towards greater maturity. Others have questions but are afraid to voice them, particularly if they seem to challenge received doctrine or established teaching. Others, still, feel that they must unquestioningly accept every item of Christian doctrine and dogma, either as a way of avoiding difficult and disturbing issues or because they have been schooled to do so. Whatever the reasons, the result is the same: faith fails to grow because it is never stretched. However strong and secure it may seem, when circumstances arise that put it to the test it will be found wanting. We all have some answers but no one has them all. Similarly, we all have some questions, even though we may refuse to admit them. Never fear those questions, still less be ashamed of them. Believe rather that God is able to use them to lead you into a deeper understanding of his purpose and a richer awareness of his love.

Activity

What's my line? (see page 81).

Reading: John 3:1-6, 9-10; 19:38-42

Now there was a Pharisee named Nicodemus, a leader of the Jews. He came to Jesus by night and said to him, 'Rabbi, we know that you are a teacher who has come from God; for no one can do these signs that you do apart from the presence of God.' Jesus answered him, 'Very truly, I tell you, no one can see the kingdom of God without being born from above.' Nicodemus said to him, 'How can anyone be born after having grown old? Can one enter a second time into the mother's womb and be born?' Jesus answered, 'Very truly, I tell you, no one can enter the kingdom of God without being born of water and Spirit. What is born of the flesh is flesh, and what is born of the Spirit is spirit.' Nicodemus said to him, 'How can these things be?' Jesus answered him, 'Are you a teacher of Israel, and yet you do not understand these things?'

(Later, following the death of Jesus, we read)

Joseph of Arimathea, who was a disciple of Jesus, though a secret one because of his fear of the Jews, asked Pilate to let him take away the body of Jesus. Pilate gave him permission; so he came and removed his body. Nicodemus, who had at first come to Jesus by night, also came, bringing a mixture of myrrh and aloes, weighing about a hundred pounds. They took the body of Jesus and wrapped it with the spices in linen cloths, according to the burial custom of the Jews. Now there was a garden in the place where he was crucified, and in the garden there was a new tomb in which no one had ever been laid. And so, because it was the Jewish day of Preparation, and the tomb was nearby, they laid Jesus there. *(NRSV)*

Comment

Is it right to question faith? It all depends on the question, you may reply, and you will be right, for, as we will see in this course, there are various kinds of questions we may ask, not all of them necessarily of value. I do not want to pre-empt those now, but consider, if you will, two contrasting ways in which we might

15

query something. One might be along the lines, 'Can you enlarge on that a little? Could you explain in more detail? Would you mind telling me more?' We might find such questions asked in an enquirers' class for baptism or confirmation, someone having come to faith and wanting to find out more about it, eager to learn and to grow as a Christian. All of us, no doubt, would applaud questions such as those, our only regret being perhaps that we tend to lose that enthusiasm and hunger as we become more established in discipleship. The other kind of query is very different. 'That doesn't make sense,' we might say; 'how can it be?' Or perhaps, 'I'd like to believe it, but how does it fit with the world as I know it?' Are questions like these equally permissible for the Christian, or are they to be quashed, avoided, shunned or ignored? Is asking them a sign of strength or weakness, of faith or doubt, of commitment or compromise?

The story of Nicodemus revolves around both sorts of questions. He saw in Jesus something special, someone who spoke with the unmistakable authority of God, and he wanted to find out more, so, risking the censure of his fellow Pharisees, he approached Jesus under cover of darkness. It couldn't have been easy to do that, for it meant questioning the tradition he had been schooled in, putting himself out of step with his colleagues, and he knew, should they get to hear of his meeting, that he could expect short shrift from any of them. Yet he had listened to Jesus and felt challenged both by the man and his message. So he came and he talked, and as the conversation unfolded so his questions were quick to surface. 'I tell you,' said Jesus, 'no one can see the kingdom of God without being born from above.' We, today, with the benefit of hindsight may know what he's talking about, but Nicodemus had no idea. 'How can anyone be born after having grown old?' he asks. 'Can one enter a second time into the mother's womb and be born? . . . How can these things be?' (John 3:4, 9, *NRSV*). To Nicodemus, the words of Jesus just don't make sense.

Were these empty idle questions, indicative of doubt or scepticism? Of course not! On the contrary, they reveal someone willing to ask and keep on asking; to seek until he has found. Nicodemus was hungry and thirsty for truth, and so long as things weren't clear he was determined to continue searching for enlightenment. That must have required considerable courage and humility, for as a religious 'expert', an individual schooled in the Law and the Prophets, Nicodemus by rights should have known and understood what Jesus was talking about. As the latter pointedly observed, 'Are you a teacher of Israel, and yet you do not understand these things?' To admit that he didn't know, that he needed further instruction from an itinerant teacher with no recognised authority of his own, must have taken some doing. Yet he came, and he asked, and he asked again, refusing to settle for just part of the picture.

To me, what we see here is Nicodemus putting into practice the advice given in the book of Proverbs, 'to . . . cry out for insight . . . raise your voice for understanding . . . [and] . . . search for it as for hidden treasures' (Proverbs 2:3, 4, *NRSV*). He recognised that true wisdom, or knowledge of God, does not come automatically but must be searched for and worked at, and in his case that meant asking until he received, seeking until he found.

We see another parallel in the questions asked by young children. As any parent will know, 'why' is a word that very quickly establishes itself in a toddler's vocabulary. During the early years of childhood, every story, every conversation, every moment seems to be punctuated by that one insistent question. It can be exhausting, even occasionally infuriating, but, of course, it is an essential part of growing up and the sign of a healthy enquiring mind. Children not only *want* to know more about the world around them; they *need* to know. The number of questions may moderate with time, but a willingness to wrestle with questions continues to be important throughout our lives. Indeed, it is precisely this that lies behind every discovery and advance in human knowledge we might care to mention. So it is also with faith. Unless we are ready to ask concerning the things we do not know or understand, we will never find answers or move on to new insights and understanding. That is not to say all questions are useful – they can be abused like anything else – but if we ask honestly they can be a vital step towards growth in Christian maturity.

Do you still ask questions of your faith, looking to progress along the road of discipleship? Have you the eager enquiring mind of a new believer, hungry to learn more of Christ and to grow in understanding? Are you constantly seeking fresh insights and new horizons; as Paul put it, to comprehend 'what is the breadth and length and height and depth, and to know the love of Christ that surpasses knowledge, so that you may be filled with all the fullness of God' (Ephesians 3:18-19, *NRSV*)? As Christians, we should always be moving forward into uncharted territory, for, however established our faith, there is always more to learn and more to discover. Is that true of us, or have we become casual, complacent, apathetic? Never be afraid to ask questions, even if it means challenging what others have told you or questioning God himself. To cling rigidly to our views come what may is a sign of uncertainty not belief, of insecurity rather than confidence. It is those who are unsure of themselves who shout the loudest about their opinions; those who are uneasy about their own position that refuse to admit they might have got things wrong. A faith rooted in a living, personal experience of God's love will be able to bring before him, freely and openly, the things we do not know or understand.

We are not told how the meeting between Nicodemus and Jesus ended, but a small detail towards the end of John's Gospel suggests that it may have proved fruitful. Together with Joseph of Arimathea, Nicodemus went to Pilate following the death of Jesus and requested permission to take away and bury the body. Is it reading too much into this to suggest that Nicodemus had come to faith? I don't think so; John himself, I believe, intends us to assume just that through his description of Nicodemus as one 'who had at first come to Jesus by night'. He had come initially under cover of darkness, in secret for fear of the consequences. Now he came openly, nailing his colours to the mast, having seen the light. No doubt he still had questions, much that he did not understand, but it appears he had come to regard himself not just as an enquirer but as a follower, doing what he could to respond in faith. He'd asked, he'd listened and he'd found. Are we ready to do the same?

Summary

- Is it right to ask questions? Most of us will applaud the eagerness of an enquirer, keen to learn more about faith, but how far should our questions go?

- Nicodemus came to Jesus wanting to know more, but also having many questions concerning things he found difficult to understand or accept. He recognised in Jesus someone who spoke and acted with God's authority, but as the conversation developed he became increasingly confused, unable to grasp what was being said.

- To admit that he didn't understand couldn't have been easy. As a Pharisee, Nicodemus was expected not simply to have a grasp of spiritual matters but to be an expert in them. Yet he knew that unless he voiced his questions he would not find the answers he was looking for.

- In his coming to Jesus and willingness to question, Nicodemus acted upon words from Proverbs that urge us to search for wisdom as for hidden treasure. We can draw an analogy with the way young children repeatedly ask 'why?' – always wanting to make sense of their experience and resolve their questions. Similarly, as we progress along the path of Christian discipleship, we sometimes need to ask questions concerning things we don't understand. This is a sign of health and an important step towards reaching Christian maturity.

- Are we still eager to learn more of Christ? A willingness to question is not a sign of insecurity but of confidence in God's loving purpose. It is because we trust that we feel able to explore more deeply.

- We are not told the outcome of Nicodemus' encounter with Jesus but the fact that he later went with Joseph of Arimathea to ask for the body of Jesus suggests that his questions had been answered and that he had come to faith. Are we ready to follow his example of seeking until we find?

Discussion

- What place do you see for questions in the Christian life? How important is it to have an enquiring mind? Are there dangers associated with this?

- Are you still as eager to learn more about faith as you once were? What might stop you from being so, and what can you do about it if you're not?

- Do you feel that sufficient room is made within the Church for questions? What sort of questions are considered acceptable and unacceptable? Have you ever felt isolated or guilty because there are aspects of the gospel you don't understand or find hard to accept?

Prayer

Gracious God,
    we thank you for all you have revealed to us in Christ
    and for the faith you have put in our hearts,
    but we thank you also that there is more to understand
    in our continuing journey of discovery.
We bring you, then, the things we cannot make sense of,
    the events of life that baffle and bemuse,
    the questions we struggle to answer.
We bring you our certainty and uncertainty,
    those areas where faith is sure
    and those where it hangs by a thread.
Give us sufficient trust to acknowledge our questions openly
    and to offer them honestly to you in prayer,
    confident that they are a part of faith,
    able to lead us to new insights
    and a deeper understanding of your purpose,
    and to enrich our experience of your grace.
Through Jesus Christ our Lord.
Amen.

Meditation of Nicodemus

It was dark when I went to him that first time,
    the middle of the night when all was quiet –
    and can you blame me?
It just wouldn't have done, would it,
    a man in my position to be seen associating with Jesus? –
    even a hint of involvement
    and my fellow Pharisees would have lynched me on the spot!
He was the enemy,
    the blasphemer,
    the one who threatened everything we stood for –
    not just misguided,
    but dangerous,
    evil –
    a threat to our society,
    a challenge to the very heart of our religion.
I knew all that,
    or at least I knew the theory,
    and yes, I'd been as shocked as any
    by some of the things he'd said,
    not to mention the things he'd done.
Yet I couldn't get him out of my mind, try as I might.
I can't say why exactly,
    for it wasn't any one word or deed that hooked me –
    it was all of them together,
    the way each reinforced the other,
    combining to make him the person he was.
He spoke of love,
    and he showed what love was all about.
He talked of forgiveness,
    and I simply haven't met a more forgiving man.
He talked of life,
    and there was a quality to his that I couldn't help but envy.
He talked of God,
    and I could see God was more real,

more personal,
more special to him,
than I'd ever have dreamed possible for anyone.
So I went
and I talked.
I listened
and I learned,
though I was nervous,
hesitant,
strictly incognito,
and so very, very slow to understand.
Yet little by little the truth broke through my confusion,
a ray of light in the darkness,
new birth for my parched and barren soul.

It was dark when I went again,
a night far blacker than that first,
for they'd taken their revenge by then as I knew they would,
done him to death on the cross.
And as he hung there in agony,
his gasps piercing the air,
suddenly the sun vanished and darkness fell.
That had them worried, you can well imagine,
more than a few scuttling off in panic.
But not me,
for I had seen the truth he spoke of
and found the life he promised.
So while others stumbled blindly in the darkness,
for me it was lighter than the lightest day,
and brighter than the brightest sunshine.

Further reading: Proverbs 2:3-6

If you indeed cry out for insight, and raise your voice for under-standing, if you seek it like silver and search for it as for hidden treasures – then you will understand the fear of the Lord and find the knowledge of God. For the Lord gives wisdom; from his mouth come knowledge and understanding. (*NRSV*)

Suggestions for action

If there are areas of faith where you have questions, talk to someone honestly about them. Don't expect immediate answers, but don't be afraid to admit there are some things you are unsure of. If you have become casual in discipleship, take time to read some devotional or study material, preferably something reflecting traditions and perspectives other than your own, so that it might challenge you to think more deeply about your faith.

Closing prayer

Gracious God,
    give me courage to ask questions,
    faith to live with them,
    and grace to grow through them,
    to the glory of your name.
Amen.

Second week
Disturbing questions

Opening prayer

Holy God, give me true faith in you.
In times of doubt and questioning,
   when my belief is confused by new learning,
   new teaching, new thought,
   when my faith is strained by creeds, by doctrines,
   by mysteries beyond my understanding,
   give me the faithfulness of a disciple
   and the courage of a believer in you;
   give me confidence to examine,
   and faith to trust in, all truth;
   stability to hold fast to what is good,
   with the benefit of new insights and interpretations;
   to acknowledge when fresh truth has been revealed to me,
   and in troublesome times genuinely to grasp new knowledge
   and to combine it loyally and honestly with the old;
   give me the insight to refrain
   both from stubborn rejection of new revelations
   and from the easy assumption that mine
   is a more enlightened generation.
Save me and help me,
I humbly pray, O Lord.
Amen.

George Ridding

Introduction

There are times, aren't there, when our faith is thrown into confusion, when, instead of being secure in what we believe, we find ourselves wrestling with doubt? Such moments are often compounded by a sense of guilt, an uneasy feeling that it is wrong to entertain such thoughts. Yet, much though we wish the questions weren't there, we cannot avoid them, any attempt to brush them aside proving futile. Many factors may cause such a time and several issues be involved – the apparent triumph of evil over good, a personal crisis or disappointment, disillusionment with the Church, to name but some – but perhaps the greatest challenge to faith lies for most in the problem of suffering. How is it, we ask, that a supposedly loving and caring God can allow so much pain and misery to rack our world? How can such a God stand by while a loved one is taken from us, while a child is struck by cancer, while innocent people are slaughtered, while thousands every day die of starvation? If there is one thing non-Christians will point to as an argument against God it is this, and the disturbing thing is that sometimes we find it hard not to agree with them. Across the centuries, people have wrestled with this conundrum yet failed to come up with wholly satisfactory solutions. Some offer pat answers that serve only to add to the misery of those wrestling with inexplicable suffering.

The aim of this session is not to propose another theory or explanation. Rather, it is to emphasise that tackling the issue and wrestling with the questions it may raise is not a sign of doubt but faith. It may not sometimes feel like it – indeed, it may seem quite the opposite – but sometimes facing the question is as important as finding the answer. If faith is to grow, it has to find a place for both.

Activity
Riddle (see page 81).

Reading: Psalm 10:1; 22:1-2; Job 3:11, 20-21a

Why, O Lord, are you so distant? Why do you hide yourself from me in my hour of need? My God, my God, why have you abandoned me? Why are you so far from helping me, from heeding my groans? I cry to you by day, O God, but you do not answer; and by night, but gain no respite . . . Why did I not die at birth, expire when I was brought from my mother's womb? Why do those consumed by despair continue to see the light of day, and why is life given to the bitter in soul who long for death only for it not to come?

Comment

Many years back, I came across a book with the title *The Faith to Doubt*. I wanted to read more immediately, for the title alone spoke volumes. Instead of pitting doubt against faith, as is so often done, it suggested that they are two sides of the one coin, both belonging together and each requiring the other. To me, that was a liberating truth, for, like many others, I had wrestled with a sense of guilt at questioning areas of my faith, feeling that I was somehow failing God through even entertaining the possibility of doubt. For many, that anxiety is compounded by the fear that other Christians will condemn them for not having enough faith. If that isn't hard enough, perhaps most difficult of all is the inner, often unvoiced, fear of where our questions might lead; a secret dread that if we follow them through they might challenge, and perhaps even destroy, long-cherished convictions. All kinds of deep-rooted fears may cause us to hide our questions and deny our doubts even to ourselves, or to brood over them in guilty silence.

If any of that rings bells for you, then look, if you haven't done already, at the book of Job, for in his story you will find many of your questions echoed. It begins with a picture of quiet contentment, Job wealthy and happy, surrounded by a loving family and all the material trappings of success. His tranquillity, however, was soon to be rudely shattered as, out of the blue, disaster struck: his live-stock stolen by bandits, his family killed during a violent storm, and finally Job himself contracting some dreadful disease that left his body covered in suppurating sores, unrecognisable to family and friends alike. Little wonder, then, that Job started to question what was going on. 'Why did I not die at birth, expire when I was brought from my mother's womb? Why do those consumed by despair continue to see the light of day, and why is life given to the bitter in soul who long for death only for it not to come?' The words of someone mystified by the events of life, overwhelmed by calamity, driven so close to the edge of despair that he finally began to wrestle with God himself, and as he struggled to make sense of it all, so the questions became more intense, desperate and rebellious. 'I will not restrain my mouth, I will speak in the anguish of my spirit; I will complain in the bitterness of my soul . . . If I sin, what do I do to you, you watcher of humanity? Why have you made me your target? Why have I become a burden to you? Why do you not pardon my transgression and take away my iniquity?' (Job 7:11, 20-21a, *NRSV*).

Have you ever spoken to God like that, perhaps in more temperate language yet nonetheless voicing your frustration and despair? Or does the very idea shock you? It did Job's three friends, Bildad, Eliphaz and Zophar, each of them scandalised by what they saw as his lack of faith. How dare he question God's justice? How could he suggest that established teaching might be wrong? Yet Job was past caring what others might think. He wanted answers. He needed to know what God was playing at, to come to terms with his experiences, and to make sense of his faith.

Was he wrong to ask such questions? Well, if he was, he was by no means the only person in the Bible to do so. The book of Ecclesiastes contains equally forthright questions, and, perhaps more surprisingly, so too do the Psalms. 'Why, O Lord, are you so distant? Why do you hide yourself from me in my hour of need? . . . How much longer, Lord? Will you keep on forgetting me always? How much longer will you conceal yourself from me? How much longer must I endure this ache in my soul, and this wretchedness in my heart throughout the day? How much longer will my enemy lord it over me. Lord God, pay heed and answer me . . . My God, my God, why have you abandoned me? Why are you so far from helping me, from heeding my groans? I cry to you by day, O God, but you do not answer; and by night, but gain no respite' (Psalm 10:1; Psalm 13:1-3a; Psalm 22:1-2). So I could continue. There is no pulling of punches here, no qualms in berating God, challenging his justice and searching for answers. Yet, of course, the Psalms also include some of the greatest songs of praise and most wonderful expressions of faith ever written. At one moment, they brim over with joy, effervesce with thanksgiving, explode into jubilant praise, but a moment later we find the psalm writers brooding over things that left them feeling puzzled, confused, lost, angry and even abandoned. The key point is this: they were not afraid to voice their questions, to ask God what was happening, even to tell God to his face that life failed sometimes to square with faith.

Such questions do not indicate a compromising of their convictions or betrayal of their faith. On the contrary, the psalm writers, like Job, posed them not because they didn't believe but because they did! If they hadn't understood God to be just and righteous there would have been no difficulty. If they hadn't seen him as loving and compassionate there would have been no mystery, no puzzle to solve. It was because they believed those things that they felt constrained to voice their doubts, and the important thing to recognise is that God understood their predicament. He didn't reject those who dared to question him. He didn't tell them that they ought to have more faith. Instead, in his own way and time, he led them into a deeper understanding of his purpose and a fuller appreciation of his love. Far from doubt destroying faith, it was faith that allowed doubt in the first place and that opened the way for them to grow through their questions.

Do the Psalms or the book of Job give an answer to the problem of suffering? I wish they did, but sadly there are no simple solutions. Essentially, the answer Job came away with is that we are dealing here with matters that are beyond us, that defy explanation in terms of this life – an idea we will look at in more detail in our final session. Job was written not to offer a catch-all explanation of suffering but to counter the simplistic interpretations prevalent in his day. Yet that's not quite the end of the story. For one thing, it was Job, with all his doubts and questions, rather than his three friends, with their pat answers and rigid orthodoxy, who was commended by God – Job who had the temerity to question orthodox teaching and to challenge accepted tenets of faith. 'My wrath is kindled against you and against your two friends', says God to Eliphaz, 'for you have not spoken of me what is right, as my servant Job has' (Job 42:7b, *NRSV*). Unlike them, Job refused unthinkingly to accept established teaching when everything he experienced contradicted it. He had sufficient courage to think for himself and to work out his faith in the context of life as he knew it. He didn't argue for the sake of arguing but because he wanted to make sense of his faith and to hold on to it whatever he might face. 'I would lay my case before him, and fill my mouth with arguments. I would learn what he would answer me, and understand what he would say to me' (Job 23:4, *NRSV*).

Secondly, alongside the doubts and questions, Job held on to faith in God's purpose. 'He knows the way that I take; when he has tested me, I shall come out like gold' (23:10, *NRSV*). Despite all he faced, Job remained convinced that God was with him and that, in some way unbeknown to him, when he finally emerged from the darkness he would be a stronger person for it. Though he couldn't explain his suffering, and though he longed for it to end, he believed that God was using it to deepen his faith and draw him closer to himself. Don't think I'm suggesting here an easy answer to suffering after all, for I'm not. What Job is saying is that it can be constructive rather than destructive, helping us to see a new dimension to life and to grow as people. It's easy to theorise in such terms, much harder to think like that when we are the one suffering; a fact which makes Job's testimony all the more remarkable.

If we truly seek answers, though, we must turn ultimately to the cross and to the agony endured there by Jesus. Even here the questions remain – the crucifixion if anything serving to deepen rather than unravel the mystery of suffering – but in the crucified Christ we see a God who not only understands our pain but also identifies with it, enduring it himself to bring us life.

For us all, at some time, questions will come; moments of doubt and uncertainty, of painful searching after truth. We should not be ashamed of such times, still less pretend that they don't exist. We have a God who understands us even when we don't understand him, who is with us even though he may seem distant; who is able to lead us through the night of doubt and sorrow into a new dawn. Hidden away and denied, doubt will inexorably eat away our faith. Acknowledged and faced openly, God can use it to deepen our trust and open our lives to a fuller appreciation of his love. I can't prove that, and I may well at times question it, but thankfully God accepts both faith and doubt, recognising them as two halves of one whole, even if we don't.

Summary

- Many people feel guilty about asking questions concerning their faith, fearing that doubt may be construed as a sign of faithlessness. They see doubt as the opposite of faith rather than integral to it. As a result, we often deny or hide our questions rather than openly admit them.

- The Bible, however, contains many searching questions, nowhere more so than in the book of Job. Overwhelmed by tragedy and suffering, Job found himself questioning traditional teaching about God and struggling to reconcile faith with life.

- Job's friends were shocked at his temerity in voicing questions, but he didn't care. His only concern was to make sense of his experiences.

- The psalm writers were similarly unafraid to challenge God when life seemed at odds with faith. Although the Psalms contain some of the greatest expressions of faith they also contain some of the most direct and searching questions in the Bible.

- Such questioning did not reflect a lack of faith but arose directly from it. Because Job and the psalm writers found it difficult sometimes to reconcile their experiences with their convictions about God, they felt the need to probe deeper. Far from undermining faith, doubt reflected a determination to strengthen it.
- Neither the book of Job nor the Psalms offer simple answers to the question of suffering. The conclusion reached in Job seems to be that we simply cannot know the ways of God.
- Furthermore, Job held firm to the conviction that God was with him in his suffering, even though he couldn't understand it. He believed that he would emerge the stronger for what he had been through. This doesn't offer a complete answer, but perhaps enables us to find some meaning in suffering. For the Christian, some kind of answer, albeit one that still leaves many questions, is found in the cross and the knowledge that God was willing to suffer in Christ for us.
- All of us will probably experience doubt at some time, faced by the vicissitudes of life. If we deny that doubt or hide from it, it will eat away at and destroy our faith. If we openly acknowledge doubt, God is able to use it to help us grow in faith.

Discussion

- Are there times when you have felt overwhelmed by questions, unable to reconcile a God of love with suffering that you or your loved ones have faced?
- Are there particular aspects of Christian belief that you find hard to understand or accept? What are these? Where do your difficulties lie?
- Do you see doubt as something positive or negative? Do you think it makes sense to talk of having the faith to doubt?

Prayer

Living God,
> there is so much suffering in this world of ours,
> so much pain, sorrow and evil.

It is hard sometimes to reconcile all this with it being your world too,
> created by you and precious in your sight.

We search desperately for answers,
> clinging first to this and then to that,
> and underneath there are times when our faith begins to crumble.

Teach us, though we cannot always see it,
> that you are there,
> sharing in our anguish,
> carrying in yourself the agony of creation
> as it groans under the weight of imperfection.

Teach us that you will not rest
> until that day when all suffering is ended,
> when evil is no more
> and your kingdom is established;
> and in that assurance give us strength to face each day,
> whatever it might bring.

Amen.

Meditation

(This meditation puts us in the shoes of someone struggling to make sense of faith in the light of the suffering that surrounds us each day.)

Why, Lord?

I know I shouldn't ask that, but I just can't help it,
> for I'm troubled,
> unable to make sense of this faith of mine,
> unable to make sense of anything.

It doesn't worry me usually,
> for I can avoid the issues, thankful they don't touch me –
> not *yet* anyway.

But today I've been surrounded by suffering,
    by the sheer weight of human need,
    and it's got to me in a way it rarely has before.
I visited the hospital,
    and saw my friend there in the cancer ward curled up in bed,
    eyes sunken,
    teeth gritted against the pain –
    the operation over, but the prognosis grim.
I left him, blinking back the tears,
    but there were others, so many others,
    looking across the ward at me with pain,
    fear and sorrow in their eyes.
I went on to the nursing home to see another friend,
    once so vibrant, so full of life,
    but now her mind gone, her body withered –
    a mocking shadow of her former self,
    waiting for the merciful release of death.
I was glad to leave, Lord,
    glad to get out into the fresh air away from it all;
    but then an ambulance raced past, sirens blaring,
    a drunken vagrant stumbled by the roadside,
    and across the street a young boy grimaced in a wheelchair,
    limbs twisted, mouth dribbling.
It was everywhere,
    human suffering crying out in defiant protest –
    on the front of the newspaper, the car radio, the television news –
    another murder, another rape, another war, another tragedy;
    and suddenly Lord, as I stared starkly into the darkness,
    I could hold it back no longer,
    the inevitable question:
    why?

My child,
    don't be ashamed of asking,
    for I don't blame you,
    not in the slightest.

On the contrary, my only surprise is that it took you so long,
    for it's not as it should be, this world I've made,
    not as I want it,
    nor as I planned it.
I look upon it day after day,
    the pain and sorrow,
    the hatred and cruelty,
    and it breaks my heart to see the beauty I intended
    so cruelly disfigured,
    laughter turning to despair,
    joy into tragedy.
That's why I came through my Son,
    sharing your humanity and bearing your sorrow –
    to ensure that one day it will be different,
    the time coming when there will be no more suffering,
    tears or darkness.
It *will* come, believe me,
    but the time must be right,
    and until then as well as joy there must be sorrow,
    as well as pleasure, pain,
    as well as life, death,
    each a part of a fallen, broken world.
Yet seen or unseen,
    recognised or unrecognised,
    I am there with you,
    not watching from the sidelines, casually aloof,
    nor safely at a distance, untouched and unmoved,
    but sharing in your hurt,
    aching with those who ache,
    groaning with those who groan,
    weeping with those who weep.
I cannot remove your pain,
    but I can help bear it,
    and though you'll still have doubts and still ask why,
    I can only say, hold on to me,
    as I keep hold of you.

Further reading: Isaiah 53:4-6

Surely he has carried our weaknesses and bore our afflictions; yet we reckoned him stricken, struck down and afflicted by God. He was wounded, though, for our misdeeds, crushed for our mistakes; he endured the punishment that made us whole and his bruises brought us healing. We have all gone astray like sheep, each going our own way, but the Lord has laid on him the offences of us all.

Suggestions for action

Open your heart to God, and share with him your questions as well as your faith. Be honest with him about your doubts. Face them, and talk them through with others.

Closing prayer

Sovereign God,
    in the puzzles and mysteries of life,
    and in all that seems to contradict my faith,
    help me to believe still that you are there
    and that your purpose will not be defeated.
Amen.

Third week

The faith in question

Opening prayer

I ask you, O God, the God of truth,
    that what I ought to know you will teach me,
    that where I am mistaken you will correct me,
    that whenever I stumble you will support me,
    and from all that is false,
    all that is damaging,
    you will always protect me.
Amen.

Brooke Foss Westcott

Introduction

'Why do you ask?' That can be a disconcerting question, can't it? One moment, we're doing the asking, and then, before we know it, the tables are turned so that we're the ones under the spotlight. The query may be put for a variety of motives. Sometimes it is simply a device to deflect an awkward question that has struck a little too near the mark. Sometimes, it is a way of finding out if we know more than we're letting on. Equally, it may merely reflect a genuine interest in our reason for asking. Similarly, our answer may obscure as much as it reveals. 'No reason,' we might say, when in fact we're thirsting to hear the latest piece of gossip or to confirm some snippet we've recently heard on the grapevine. 'Just curious,' we may murmur, when the truth is that we're cunningly trying to steer the conversation in a particular direction. Questions are not always what they seem, ulterior motives frequently lying behind them.

The same may be true in the context of faith. In the last session, we saw that questions have a very real place in Christian discipleship, able to lead us to a deeper understanding of God and his activity in the world, but, like every good thing, they can be abused. We can fall into the trap of asking for the sake of it, of becoming so full of our own cleverness that we pick holes in and quibble over incidental details rather than focus on the essentials of the gospel. Such an attitude eventually undermines our faith, corroding commitment until it wears dangerously thin. Like many of those who questioned Jesus during his ministry, we can end up looking for excuses not to believe, cynicism and doubt feeding on their own fruits. Those who genuinely search for truth will, I believe, find the answers they seek. Those who simply indulge in speculation, or who raise trivial questions in order to sidestep challenges they would rather not face, may find themselves caught up eventually in a web of their own making from which it proves hard to escape.

Activity

Trivial Pursuit™ (see page 82).

Reading: Mark 12:13-34

Then they sent to him some Pharisees and some Herodians to trap him in what he said. And they came and said to him, 'Teacher, we know that you are sincere, and show deference to no one; for you do not regard people with partiality, but teach the way of God in accordance with truth. Is it lawful to pay taxes to the emperor or not? Should we pay them, or should we not?' But knowing their hypocrisy, he said to them, 'Why are you putting me to the test? Bring me a denarius and let me see it.' And they brought one. Then he said to them, 'Whose head is this, and whose title?' They

37

answered, 'The emperor's.' Jesus said to them, 'Give to the emperor the things that are the emperor's, and to God the things that are God's.' And they were utterly amazed at him.

Some Sadducees, who say there is no resurrection, came to him and asked him a question, saying, 'Teacher, Moses wrote for us that if a man's brother dies, leaving a wife but no child, the man shall marry the widow and raise up children for his brother. There were seven brothers; the first married and, when he died, left no children; and the second married her and died, leaving no children; and the third likewise; none of the seven left children. Last of all, the woman herself died. In the resurrection whose wife will she be? For the seven had married her.'

Jesus said to them, 'Is not this the reason you are wrong, that you know neither the scriptures nor the power of God? For when they rise from the dead, they neither marry nor are given in marriage, but are like angels in heaven. And as for the dead being raised, have you not read in the book of Moses, in the story about the bush, how God said to him, "I am the God of Abraham, the God of Isaac, and the God of Jacob"? He is God not of the dead, but of the living; you are quite wrong.'

One of the scribes came near and heard them disputing with one another, and seeing that he answered them well, he asked him, 'Which commandment is the first of all?' Jesus answered, 'The first is, "Hear, O Israel: the Lord our God, the Lord is one; you shall love the Lord your God with all your heart, and with all your soul, and with all your mind, and with all your strength." The second is this, "You shall love your neighbour as yourself." There is no other commandment greater than these.' Then the scribe said to him, 'You are right, Teacher; you have truly said that "he is one, and besides him there is no other"; and "to love him with all the heart, and with all the understanding, and with all the strength", and "to love one's neighbour as oneself" – this is much more important than all whole burnt offerings and sacrifices.' When Jesus saw that he answered wisely, he said to him, 'You are not far from the kingdom of God.' After that no one dared to ask him any question. (*NRSV*)

Comment

'Is this the right room for an argument?' So began a celebrated sketch in the BBC comedy series, *Monty Python's Flying Circus*. Not only was it hilarious in its own right, but it also brilliantly parodied the pretentiousness of much intellectual debate, argument at times being engaged in for argument's sake. I had a taste of that during my time in Oxford, the hothouse atmosphere of university life sometimes giving rise to the most impassioned of debates on what were ultimately the most trivial of subjects. Indeed, I couldn't help feeling the same about some of the research being undertaken there, including my own, the subject of many students' theses obscure to say the least. The response of the average person in the street, confronted by such high-flown disputation would, I suspect, be along the lines, 'Who cares, anyway!'

All this is not intended to disparage learning, still less to suggest it should not be applied to the Christian faith. When I read about and hear Christians casually dismissing scientific research and biblical scholarship as though they are of no consequence, I sometimes despair, for such a response serves only to alienate non-Christians from the Church and the gospel. Some questions *need* to be asked and will not go away, however much we may pretend they are not there. Others, though, are different, asked to avoid an issue, to put people down, to create a smokescreen or simply to show off one's own cleverness in argument. Take, for example, Prime Minister's Question Time or a debate in the House of Commons. Certain questions are tabled for the sole purpose of point scoring, designed to find fault, humiliate and gloat over failures. Others are rhetorical, affording government ministers an opportunity to preen themselves on their successes. Others, still, aim to draw attention away from contentious issues, perhaps taking the heat off a beleaguered colleague, while others again seek precisely the opposite, hoping to catch individuals on the hop and thus lure them into an embarrassing blunder. Only a few questions are asked for the purpose of enlightenment, with any genuine interest in the answer.

So it can be with questions of faith, as is graphically illustrated in our reading above. First, the Pharisees came with a question – 'Is it lawful to pay taxes to the emperor or not?' – and in case we might miss the motivation behind their enquiry, Mark spells it out for us. The intention was to trap Jesus into an indiscretion, to cause him to say something that might be construed as subversive so that they could bring a charge against him before the Roman authorities. Should he avoid this pitfall by saying it is lawful to pay taxes to Caesar, another was waiting for him, for he could be accused of collaborating with the enemy, compromising the principles of his faith for the sake of expediency. It looked like a Catch-22 situation, both options equally unappealing, yet, in a deft stroke, Jesus turned the tables on them, seeing through their subterfuge and coming up with a reply that left onlookers rubbing their heads in amazement. 'Give to the emperor the things that are the emperor's, and to God the things that are God's.' In other words, 'It's not for me to tell you; make up your own minds before God.'

Next came the Sadducees, and again the object of their question was clear. Fiercely critical of teaching concerning resurrection, they wanted to prove their point in public and to hold anything Jesus might have to say on the subject up to ridicule. So they came with a long and convoluted question concerning a hypothetical situation that might emerge following the resurrection, a situation that, to them, exposed the absurdity of the whole idea. Ironically, the question makes a fair point, for though the scenario painted is admittedly unlikely it is nonetheless possible (we will look more at issues of this sort in session five of this book), but here it wasn't a genuine question at all but another barely disguised attempt to make Jesus look a fool. Once again, however, Jesus turned the tables on questioners. The rabbinical-type exchange of ideas is somewhat difficult for us to understand today, but essentially, in answering their question, he played them at their own game, quoting a passage of scriptures central to their teaching but one that he interpreted in an altogether different way. If it makes sense, he tells them, to speak of the God of Abraham, Isaac and Jacob, then surely he must be the God of the living! Of course, what he meant by this was nothing like the Sadducees' understanding, but if they tried to argue with him they would come perilously close to undermining teaching concerning the importance of the patriarchs that lay at the heart of their tradition. It was a masterstroke, which once again silenced his critics.

Finally, there came a scribe, a teacher of the law – in other words, another member of the religious establishment – but this time it is harder to gauge the reason behind the question. 'Of all the commandments,' he asked, 'which is the most important?' (Mark 12:28). Was this simply another attempt to ensnare Jesus? Perhaps it was, perhaps it wasn't – it's hard to tell. Many commentators believe it was genuinely asked, the scribe impressed by the way Jesus had tackled the queries put to him and in consequence eager to hear his views on the Jewish law. To a point, I think that's true, but there may have been more to it than that. The question he raised had long been a subject of debate in rabbinic schools, and the scribe clearly felt he knew the answer. Is this why he raised the issue in the first place – to reinforce his opinion and parade his credentials before Jesus – or is that being a bit harsh? I'm not sure, but given the context in this chapter and the fact that no one after this encounter dared question Jesus further, it's perfectly possible. What is sure is that he never expected what followed. 'You are right, Teacher', he said, after Jesus highlighted the first two commandments as the most important; 'you have truly said that "he is one, and besides him there is no other"; and "to love him with all the heart, and with all the understanding, and with all the strength", and "to love one's neighbour as oneself" – this is much more important than all whole burnt offerings and sacrifices.' So far, so good, the scribe more than happy to hand out plaudits, but then we read, 'When Jesus saw that he answered wisely, he said to him, "You are not far from the kingdom of God."' What, I wonder, did the scribe make of that? Surely *he* was the expert in the law, not Jesus! And as for being *not far* from the kingdom, what was that all about? Was Jesus giving a word of encouragement here on the one hand, but also a word of warning on the other? If the scribe genuinely understood that these were the most important commandments then he had indeed discovered the kingdom of God, but how real was his understanding? Had his question been a final step towards commitment, or simply a display of his own wisdom designed to bolster his ego? Having asked Jesus' opinion on one question, he may eventually have received a little more than he'd bargained on!

Different questions, with different motives behind them, but how do they relate to us? I'm not suggesting for a moment that any of us would ask questions deliberately designed to trick, prove a point or reinforce our opinion. Mostly our motives are much more genuine, yet there can be a hidden agenda nonetheless, even though we are unaware of it. Subconsciously, we can hide behind questions as a way of avoiding what we'd rather not hear, finding it easier to pick holes in incidental details rather than face up to the challenge of discipleship. Equally, questioning can become a habit, the passing of the years bringing with them a mounting cynicism that prevents us from taking anything at face value. Again, our opinions may become entrenched in a denominational or theological point of view, or a particular style of worship, so that we automatically question any idea associated with other perspectives. We can fall into the trap of arguing about trivia, or even for argument's sake, a fact that the Apostle Paul, for one, was well aware of. 'Avoid foolish controversies,' he wrote, 'and genealogies and arguments about the law, because they are unprofitable and useless' (Titus 3:9). Paul was all too aware, from bitter experience in the early Church, of how we can be drawn into complicated disputes that have little or nothing to do with the real business of being a Christian; sucked into arguments about this or that point, which, though interesting, are finally irrelevant and useless.

It's not for me or anyone else to judge the motivation behind your questions – only you can do that. What seems important for one is incidental for another; what I find confusing you may consider simple – each of us being unique individuals. There are no hard and fast rules we can lay down, no criteria by which we can label a question admissible or inadmissible, yet if questions have an important place in discipleship they also pose very real dangers.

Sometimes it is good to ask, sometimes it isn't; sometimes we are genuinely seeking enlightenment, sometimes purposely fogging the issue. From authentic enquiry to playing games is a smaller step than we might imagine. Ask questions, yes, for at times they are necessary, but ask first why you are raising them, in case, far from leading you towards answers, they are closing your mind to the one who is ultimately the answer to all.

Summary

- Questions can be asked with a variety of motives. Instead of being genuine enquiries, their primary purpose can sometimes be to prove a point, avoid an issue or put someone down.

- So it was with the questions put to Jesus in Mark 12. First the Pharisees tried to trap him, their intention solely to find grounds for condemnation. Then the Sadducees raised an issue designed to belittle the concept of resurrection. Finally, a scribe came with a question that seems to have been more genuine than the others but that may have contained an element of self-aggrandisement.

- We may not consciously ask with ulterior motives, but our questions may nonetheless reflect a hidden agenda, being subconsciously used to evade more difficult issues, to reinforce our own opinions or to put down ideas we don't agree with. More subtly, but perhaps more dangerously, we may fall into the habit of questioning anything and everything as a matter of course.

- Paul warned against being drawn into arguments and controversies that are ultimately incidental to the gospel. He knew how divisive these could be and how easily they could undermine people's faith.

- We cannot lay down rules concerning the questions we should and shouldn't ask, for we are all different. It is important, though, to consider why we ask something, and to ensure we are genuinely seeking after truth. Otherwise, our questions may prove a hindrance rather than help.

Discussion

- Are there issues you have at one time allowed to grow out of all proportion, dwelling on them to the detriment of your faith? What were these? How did you finally put them into perspective?
- What ulterior motives might lie behind the questions we ask in daily life? How far can these fairly be applied to the questions we ask of faith?
- Do we tend to ask and approach questions in a way that reinforces our own position rather than challenges it? Is this inevitable? Are there ways we might avoid it? Are we doing it now?
- Do you think we become cynical as the years pass and thus more likely to ask questions, or entrenched in our views and therefore less likely to pose them?

Prayer

Living God,
    give us wisdom to know when we need to question,
    to search for greater understanding,
    deeper awareness
    and a fuller knowledge of your love.
But help us also to recognise when questions are misplaced,
    saying more about us than you,
    obscuring rather than revealing,
    knocking down rather than building up,
    restricting rather than stretching our faith.
Teach us, at such moments, to ask questions of ourselves,
    so that we may truly seek you in spirit and in truth,
    and come to know and love you more completely,
    through the grace of our Lord Jesus Christ.
Amen.

Meditation of an onlooker as Jesus is questioned by the crowd

He was besieged, poor man,
    bombarded by a barrage of questions,
    everyone, it seemed, wanting *his* view,
    his answer,
    his opinion –
    only, of course, *he* knew better,
    sizing them up straightaway.
Oh, some wanted to know, certainly,
    genuinely looking for enlightenment,
    but most that day were simply playing,
    the only answer that interested them the one they were fishing for.
Those Pharisees, for example –
    well, we could all see what they were up to,
    their enquiry not a question but a trap,
    a scrap of bait to catch their prey.
Then the Sadducees, asking about the resurrection –
    they'd made up their minds long before,
    and they thought they had him with that teaser of theirs –
    no way anyone could unravel those tangled threads.
As for the scribe –
    I'm not so sure,
    but I tell you this,
    he went away that day quieter than when he arrived,
    and with a preoccupied look in his eyes
    as though he'd answered one question
    but uncovered another.
They thought they could catch him out,
    expose him as a fool or charlatan,
    or use him to their advantage,
    but they couldn't,
    instead tying themselves up in knots.
We were scared to question after that,
    each one of us,

even the rabbis and teachers of the law,
for we realised that whatever we asked
he'd somehow turn it back on us –
our integrity,
our reason for asking –
and, much though we wished to deny it,
we all knew that this was the real issue,
the key question that we alone could answer.

Further reading: 1 Timothy 1:3-7

I urge you, as I did when I was on my way to Macedonia, to remain in Ephesus so that you may instruct certain people not to teach any different doctrine, and not to occupy themselves with myths and endless genealogies that promote speculations rather than the divine training that is known by faith. But the aim of such instruction is love that comes from a pure heart, a good conscience, and sincere faith. Some people have deviated from these and turned to meaningless talk, desiring to be teachers of the law, without understanding either what they are saying or the things about which they make assertions. (*NRSV*)

Suggestions for action

Examine your motives behind the questions you ask concerning faith. Are you avoiding deeper issues? If so, face up to them and then see what questions remain.

Closing prayer

From thinking we have all the answers,
    and from thinking too much of questions,
    Lord, deliver us,
    in the name of Christ.
Amen.

Fourth week

Ultimate questions

Opening prayer

Lord, I believe in you:
    increase my faith.
I trust in you:
    strengthen my trust.
I love you:
    let me love you more and more.
I am sorry for my sins:
    deepen my repentance.

I worship you
    as my first beginning,
I long for you
    as my last end.
I praise you
    as my constant helper,
and call on you
    as my loving protector.

Author unknown

Introduction

Several words in the English language are overused. Terms such as 'basically', 'really', 'actually' and 'in fact' are just a few of those that are often unnecessarily employed. The word 'ultimately' is equally abused, typically meaning little more than 'finally' or 'in the end'. The true meaning of the word goes much deeper, having to do with those things that are most important, fundamental to life, of the maximum possible significance. When we speak of ultimate questions, we are talking about issues relating to good and evil, sickness and suffering, the sanctity and meaning of life, the existence of God and the possibility, if any, of life beyond death. These are questions that do not permit easy answers, yet they continue to stimulate heated debate today, just as they have always done. Why? Because they concern matters that impact directly on every one of us relating to who and what we are, why we are here, where we are going and what we can do about it.

In this session, we consider one of the most fundamental questions of all: is there a life beyond the grave? The one thing we can be sure of, it is sometimes said, is that we all die. Is that the end of the story, our faith or hope in vain, or are Christians right in affirming hope in a day of resurrection? If so, what sort of life are we talking about, what form might it take, and when and where will it be? Most people would like to believe in life after death, as can be seen from the continuing fascination exerted today by the occult, spiritualism, out-of-body experiences and the like, but many find the obstacles to belief too hard to overcome. When it comes to the afterlife, we are dealing with a question of faith like few others. In this session we ask, 'Are there any answers?'

Activity

The people in question (see page 82).

Reading: 1 Corinthians 15:12-22, 35-36, 42-44a, 50-53, 54b-57

Now if Christ is proclaimed as raised from the dead, how can some of you say there is no resurrection of the dead? If there is no resurrection of the dead, then Christ has not been raised; and if Christ has not been raised, then our proclamation has been in vain and your faith has been in vain. We are even found to be misrepresenting God, because we testified of God that he raised Christ –

whom he did not raise if it is true that the dead are not raised. For if the dead are not raised, then Christ has not been raised. If Christ has not been raised, your faith is futile and you are still in your sins. Then those also who have died in Christ have perished. If for this life only we have hoped in Christ, we are of all people most to be pitied. But in fact Christ has been raised from the dead, the first fruits of those who have died. For since death came through a human being, the resurrection of the dead also came through a human being; for as all die in Adam, so all will be made alive in Christ. But someone will ask, 'How are the dead raised? With what kind of body do they come?' Fool! What you sow does not come to life unless it dies. So it is with the resurrection of the dead. What is sown is perishable, what is raised is imperishable. It is sown in dishonour, it is raised in glory. It is sown in weakness, it is raised in power. It is sown a physical body, it is raised a spiritual body. What I am saying, brothers and sisters, is this: flesh and blood cannot inherit the kingdom of God, nor does the perishable inherit the imperishable. Listen, I will tell you a mystery! We will not all die, but we will all be changed, in a moment, in the twinkling of an eye, at the last trumpet. For the trumpet will sound, and the dead will be raised imperishable, and we will be changed. For this perishable body must put on imperishability, and this mortal body must put on immortality, then the saying that is written will be fulfilled:

'Death has been swallowed up in victory.'

'Where, O death is your victory?

Where, O death, is your sting?'

The sting of death is sin, and the power of the sin is the law. But thanks be to God, who gives us the victory, through our Lord Jesus Christ. (*NRSV*)

Comment

Do you know the hymn 'Can it be true?' It's not sung today as often as it used to be, which is a pity, for it powerfully but simply sums up the challenge of the gospel. More important for our purposes, it also sums up the questions many people want to ask of the Christian faith: 'Can it be true?' Many would like to believe, many try to and some succeed, but that insistent query is hard to silence, nagging away in innumerable minds and either impeding or undermining faith. Most people, it has to be said, have no problem accepting Jesus existed, that he was a great teacher, that he performed astonishing deeds and that he died on a cross at the hands of his enemies. The problem comes when we get to the empty tomb. Here is the point where most people shake their heads, saying, 'I'd like to believe it, but I honestly can't.'

For some the resurrection quite simply seems too good to be true. It's almost as though the very fact that the idea is so special, by definition disproves it. We are part of a world where bad rather than good news is the norm; where there's a hidden cost to every offer, nothing given for free. Good news, such as the resurrection purports to be, is dismissed as wishful thinking, delusion, hoping against hope – the stuff of daydreams rather than for hard-headed realists of the twenty-first century.

Secondly, many people want proof, some kind of evidence that the resurrection happened and that it can one day happen for them too. In a technological and scientific world, we are used to putting truths under the microscope so that they can be empirically checked and double-checked, subjected to the most rigorous of scrutiny. To be told we must accept something on faith goes against the grain. We want cast-iron certainties, not promises that we must accept on trust. We want to know how the apparent finality of death can lead on to a new chapter in our lives, a new dimension of experience.

Finally, some want to know what we mean by eternal life. Where will it be? How will we get there? When will it come? What will it be like? These and a host of other questions play on people's minds, including sometimes our own. If only we knew, we tell ourselves, faith would be so much easier. If only we could spell out the answers, we would face the vicissitudes of life now with greater confidence, as well as speak with greater assurance of the gospel to others. Yet, like the Sadducees in last week's session, albeit asking for very different reasons, the more we try to make sense of eternal life, the more of a riddle it becomes.

Where, then, does this leave us? Must we accept that faith in the resurrection is increasingly difficult to maintain in our modern-day world. Not at all! Look again at those three responses I have outlined, and you will recognise that they correspond to responses of Jesus' followers in the days immediately following his resurrection. Faith was no easier then than it is now.

Take first the idea that it's too good to be true, Christians simply convincing themselves of what they wanted to believe. The fact is that the message of the empty tomb was no more acceptable to hardheaded realists of the first century than today. When the women who had gone to anoint the body of Jesus burst in on the disciples blurting out the news that he had risen, their words, so we are told, seemed like a foolish fantasy, or, as the New International Version of the Bible so graphically puts it, 'like nonsense'. The Apostles were no credulous romantics waiting to swallow any old story, inventing the resurrection as a form of denial. They were down-to-earth individuals who had been utterly convinced that it was all over, Jesus dead and buried. Yet, each not only came to believe but also came to experience the risen presence of Christ within them through his Spirit. Was this just a delusion? Well, if it was, it had the power to change their lives, to transform them from a cowering group of disillusioned disciples into fearless ambassadors of the gospel, mingling with the crowds and proudly proclaiming their faith, willing to commit their all to Christ, even to die in his service. Can you explain that? Can you really put it down merely to wishful thinking? Certainly, when they first heard the news it did indeed seem too good to be true, but they discovered for themselves that it wasn't. Have you discovered that too?

Second, there is the question of seeking proof. Nowhere is that illustrated more clearly than in the story of Thomas, a man, rightly or wrongly, forever associated with doubt. For some reason, when the risen Christ first appeared to the disciples, he wasn't there with them, and as a result he refused to believe it had happened. Did it seem too good to be true to him also? Very possibly! Whatever his reasons, Thomas came out with those unforgettable words: 'Unless I see the mark of the nails in his hands, and put my finger in the mark of the nails and my hand in his side, I will not believe' (John 20:25b, *NRSV*) – words that I suspect many since have inwardly echoed if not outwardly expressed. Understandably, Thomas wanted proof. Wouldn't you have done in his place? Here he was in mourning and suddenly his closest friends were dancing about like newborn lambs telling him it was time to celebrate, the one he thought was dead somehow alive! It took some believing. Thomas, of course, was to be one of the lucky ones, for a week later Jesus was to appear again, and this time Thomas was there to see for himself. 'Put your finger here and see my hands. Reach out your hand and put it in my side. Do not doubt but believe' (John 20:27, *NRSV*). What would we give for an invitation like that? Only that isn't how it is today, any more than it has been for the majority of believers across history. As Jesus went on to tell Thomas, 'Blessed are those who have not seen and yet have come to believe' (John 20:29, *NRSV*). We have to live by faith, not sight. The only proof we have is the testimony of those who saw and experienced first-hand the reality of the risen Jesus. Or is it? We'll look at that more fully in a moment, but first let us turn to questions such as what, when, where and how in relation to eternal life.

We noted earlier that the Sadducees put such questions to Jesus with one aim in mind – to highlight what they saw as the impossibility of resurrection – but many people ask with very different motives, genuinely wanting to believe or to find out more. We see much the same in Paul's first letter to the church in Corinth, some Christians there clearly eager for more details as to the precise form eternal life might take. 'Someone will ask,' writes Paul, '"How are the dead raised? With what kind of body do they come?"' (1 Corinthians 15:35, *NRSV*). These are understandable questions, for the more you think about resurrection, the more complicated the issue seems to become, such that we end up tying ourselves into all kinds of knots. Can we piece together the jigsaw, working out from the various biblical clues what sort of experience resurrection might involve. Frankly, I don't think we can, for we are talking here about another world, a different dimension, an experience that, like God himself, defies description. As Paul expressed it in his triumphant words to the Corinthians, 'What I am saying, brothers and sisters, is this: flesh and blood cannot inherit the kingdom of God, nor does the perishable inherit the imperishable. Listen, I will tell you a mystery! We will not all die, but we will all be changed, in a moment, in the twinkling of an eye, at the last trumpet. For the trumpet will sound, and the dead will be raised imperishable, and we will be changed' (1 Corinthians 15:50-52). In other words, says Paul, when it comes to eternal life we are talking about another level of existence, a new kind of being, greater and more wonderful than anything we can yet conceive. Is this a cop-out, a way of avoiding the issue? Some would say so, but this brings us back to where we left off in the preceding paragraph: to the issue of where faith lies and on what it is based.

We cannot give irrefutable answers to questions concerning resurrection and eternal life, or indeed to many others relating to the things of God. We are in the realm of faith here. But is that faith dependent solely on the testimony of others, upon the biblical record of events centuries ago? The answer, of course, is no. We believe because of what we understand to be an encounter with Jesus now, an inner awareness of his presence through his Holy Spirit that sustains and nurtures us each day and that brings a new dimension to this life irrespective of what is to come. Faith is based as much on what we experience today as what God promises us tomorrow or what others have experienced yesterday. In other words, we trust in the future because of what we discover to be true in the present. Some will say we are deceiving ourselves, believing what we want to believe, interpreting life through tinted spectacles that determine what we see. There is no way we can prove they are wrong any more than they can prove they are right. It is ultimately – and I mean *ultimately* – a question of faith!

Summary

- Can it be true? That's a question many feel constrained to ask concerning the resurrection of Christ and associated teaching concerning eternal life.

- For some it's simply too good to be true. The very fact that we want to believe it suggests to people that we are deceiving ourselves, inventing the idea of resurrection as a way of denying the finality of death.

- Others want concrete proof, refusing to accept the possibility of resurrection unless indisputable grounds can be given for doing so.

- Others, still, are perplexed by questions relating to the nature of eternal life. They may wholeheartedly accept the idea of resurrection, but be disturbed and confused by their inability to picture what eternal life will be like.

- None of these responses are confined to the present day. The Apostles initially rejected the idea that Jesus had risen as nonsense. Thomas wanted proof that it had happened, and refused to believe until this was given him. Some in the church at Corinth were evidently troubled by questions relating to the nature of eternal life and the resurrection body, so much so that a few had lost faith as a result.

- Despite their initial scepticism, however, the Apostles came to believe in the resurrection, following their encounters with the risen Christ. Similarly, the doubts of Thomas were dispelled when Jesus stood in person before him. Finally, Paul called on the Corinthians to hold firmly to their faith, reminding them that when we talk of resurrection and eternal life we are dealing with a different dimension to this world.

- Questions concerning eternal life are real, yet they do not admit to irrefutable answers. Our faith is, and has to be, in things unseen. It does not, however, depend solely on the testimony of Scripture and those gone by. Above all, it is rooted in our daily experience of the risen Christ through his Holy Spirit.

- No one can prove that faith in God or eternal life is either well founded or a misguided delusion. Ultimately, it is, and must always be, a matter of faith.

Discussion

- Instead of launching straight into discussion, begin this part of this session by inviting participants to think quietly over what they see as ultimate questions in relation to faith. Encourage them to write these down, and, after sufficient time has been allowed, to share their thoughts with the rest of the group. Then allow discussion to arise naturally from the observations and comments made.
- Is your faith dependent on what happens now and on things you can see and touch? Have you tied God down to this world rather than caught through him a glimpse of the world to come?
- In what way do you picture eternal life? What form do you envisage heaven will take? Do you end up becoming tied into knots whenever you think about such things? Does that bother you?
- Would *this* life make any sense without the perspective of life to come?

Prayer

Lord,
    you call us to live by faith, not by sight.
You tell us to trust in things unseen,
    in realities we cannot grasp.
We do our best, but it's not easy,
    for we like to have everything cut and dried,
    spelt out down to the finest detail.
We struggle to cope with uncertainties

even in relation to everyday matters,
let alone in terms of our eternal destiny.
Yet deep down we know there is no other way,
for the joys you hold in store for us are beyond our imagining,
too awesome for the human mind to comprehend.
Teach us, then, to leave all things in your hands,
trusting for tomorrow through what we know of you today.
Teach us to work for your kingdom
until that day we enter into the wonder of your presence.
Amen.

Meditation of Paul

'What will it be like?' they ask me.
'What sort of body will we have? –
What sort of clothes? –
What sort of food?'
And then, as if that weren't enough,
'When will it be?
Where will we go?
How will it happen?'
As if *I* should know!
All right, so maybe I did catch a glimpse of life outside the body,
but that doesn't make me an expert, does it –
an authority on the life to come.
Yet admit that to some people and they start to question everything,
as though the whole idea of resurrection
hinges on our ability to understand it.
I know why they ask, of course I do,
for it's not easy living with mystery,
accepting claims one cannot fathom or even begin to picture,
yet is that really anything new
when it comes to the things of God?
'My thoughts are not your thoughts, nor are your ways my ways' –

isn't that what he told us? –
so why presume they are?
I realised long ago that just because we don't understand something
    doesn't mean it isn't true.
The trouble is we start in the wrong place,
    looking to what's yet to be rather than what's been already,
    but it's there that our faith rests –
    in the wonder of the empty tomb,
    the folded grave clothes, the risen Lord;
    in the glorious message of his victory over death,
    his final triumph over evil.
Isn't that enough for you?
It is for me.
I can't explain how it happened, but I know it's real,
    for I've met him myself,
    experienced his presence,
    died, through his power, to the old self and risen to the new.
Take away that, and you take away everything.
We'd all like to know more, I accept that,
    to end once and for all the guessing and speculation,
    but we wouldn't understand even if it was spelt out for us;
    the things God has in store
    being beyond the human eye to see or heart conceive.
So no more brooding about the future –
    what *may* be,
    what *could* be.
Think rather of Christ –
    what he's *done*,
    what he's *doing*,
    and then you will learn to take on trust
    the things that yet *shall* be.

Further reading: 1 Corinthians 2:9-10

No eye has seen, nor ear heard, nor any heart conceived of the things that God has prepared for those who love him. But God has revealed these things to us through the Spirit; for the Spirit explores everything, even the very depths of God's being.

Suggestions for action

If you are trying to convince yourself of the truth of resurrection through argument and reason, stop beating your head against a brick wall and recognise that we are talking here about faith. Ask yourself if you are ready to take the leap of faith necessary, either through an act of commitment or a letting go of questions.

Closing prayer

Sovereign God,
   teach us to base our faith not on what might be
   but on what *has* been and what *is*.
May all you have done and continue to do
   inspire us to trust in the future you hold for us,
   confident that as you are with us now
   so you shall be for all eternity,
   through Jesus Christ our Lord.
Amen.

Fifth week

Living with questions

Opening prayer

My God, you have created me
   to do some definite service;
   you have given some definite work to me
   which you have not given to any other.
I have my place in your plan.
I may never know what it is in this life
   but I shall be told it in the next.
Therefore I will trust you in all things.
If I am sick, my sickness may serve you.
If I am worried, my worry may serve you.
If I am in sorrow, my sorrow may serve you.
Nothing is in vain:
   all things serve a purpose.
I may lose my friends and find myself among strangers;
   I may feel forgotten so that my spirits sink;
   my future may be hidden from me;
   still, you work in all things for good,
   and I trust you.
Amen.

John Henry Newman

Introduction

Recent years have seen a considerable revival of interest in the
cultivation of herbs. Usually, we grow them simply for ornamental
and culinary purposes – to add a touch of colour and fragrance to
the garden, or an extra dash of flavour to our food. At one time,

though, herbs were grown principally for another use: for their healing and medicinal properties. The variety of ways in which herbs can be used is truly astonishing; they have served across the years as astringents, diuretics, expectorants, hypnotics, laxatives, sedatives and much else besides. In the hands of a skilled herbalist, or utilised in modern-day medicine, these qualities can all be harnessed to great effect, yet should the uninitiated attempt to treat themselves, the results could be disastrous. A book of mine at home about herbs has warnings printed in bold on nearly every page, issuing such stark advice as 'should never be collected and used for self-medication', 'should not be taken in large doses', 'should always be taken under professional supervision', 'strong doses can be toxic' or, simply, 'extremely poisonous!' The lesson is clear enough: handle with care; do not exceed a safe dose. The same herb that can cure can also kill. We need to know when we've had enough of a good thing.

The same is true when it comes to doubt and questions! In the first two sessions, I tried to show that these have a positive place in the Christian life, both able to contribute to lasting growth and health, but those same doubts and questions can equally have precisely the opposite effect. Unchecked, they can destroy our faith, estranging us from God rather than drawing us closer towards him, spreading poison deep within that inexorably undermines our spiritual health. Questions may be fair in them-selves, relating to important issues that need to be thought through, but when we focus on them at the cost of all else, that is when we run into difficulties. We need to keep a balance between what we know of God and what we don't know, between our daily experience of his love and the riddles that continue to perplex us. Dwelling on our questions and then trying to argue our way back to God is a recipe not for doubt but for disbelief, for it means putting ourselves in his place and tying him down to our limited understanding. When we place God firmly at the centre of our lives and work at cultivating our relationship with him, then, despite any misgivings we may have, we learn to live with questions until, in his time, they are resolved.

Activity

Pop-up Pirate™ (see page 83).

Reading: Mark 9:15-24

When the whole crowd saw him, they were immediately overcome with awe, and they ran forward to greet him. He asked them, 'What are you arguing about with them?' Someone from the crowd answered him, 'Teacher, I brought you my son; he has a spirit that makes him unable to speak, and whenever it seizes him, it dashes him down; and he foams and grinds his teeth and becomes rigid; and I have asked your disciples to cast it out, but they could not do so.' He answered them, 'You faithless generation, how much longer must I be among you? How much longer must I put up with you? Bring him to me.' And they brought the boy to him. When the spirit saw him, immediately it convulsed the boy, and he fell on the ground and rolled about, foaming at the mouth. Jesus asked the father, 'How long has this been happening to him?' And he said, 'From childhood. It has often cast him into the fire and into the water, to destroy him; but if you are able to do anything, have pity on us and help us.' Jesus said to him, 'If you are able! – All things can be done for the one who believes.' Immediately the father of the child cried out, 'I believe; help my unbelief!' (*NRSV*)

Comment

I talked in the Introduction to this session about herbs, but another plant can offer an equally graphic illustration of the need to keep something firmly in check. Officially, it's called *Polygonum bald-schuanicum* or Russian Vine, but the colloquial and more apt description is 'Mile-a-minute Vine', a nickname that gives a clear idea just what this plant is capable of. If you've an eyesore in your garden you want to hide or a trellis you want covering, look no further: this apparently innocuous little climber will do it in no time. The problem is that unless you're very careful, it will also cover your neighbour's trellis and rampage into every garden down your street! This plant is serious about growing, and any choicer specimen in its path had better watch out! That's not to say we shouldn't find a place for it – simply that we must make time for regularly pruning to avoid ending up with a monster on our hands.

Left unchecked, doubts and questions can similarly get out of control. They may start healthily enough – a genuine searching for understanding, a sincere striving after truth – but if we give them full rein they can take over our lives until we can think of nothing else. Inexorably, they begin to tighten their grip and strangle our faith, until we are sceptical about everything, no longer believing that answers can be found to any of our questions. Instead of having the faith to doubt, we simply have doubt without faith.

So what can we do about it? In what ways can we keep our questions under control, without falling back into the trap of feeling guilty about them, ashamed of daring to voice them? I want to focus on two passages that I believe provide the answer. The first is the incident from our reading, the father who brought his son to Jesus looking for healing. The second is the story from Matthew 14 of Peter called by Jesus to walk to him across the water. Both have one thing in common: they speak of faith *despite* doubt.

Take first the father and his epileptic son. Of all the incidents recorded in Mark, I find this story one of the easiest to relate to and hence one of the most encouraging. The father is clearly desperate, driven to despair by the increasing severity of his son's fits, but although he has come to Jesus seeking help, he clearly has doubts about what realistically he can do. '[I]f you are able to do anything,' he says, 'have pity on us and help us.' Not, 'I know you can help us' or 'just say the word and I'll be off', but '*if* you can help us' – a request loaded with doubt and hesitation. This approach is very different to that of the centurion who came on behalf of his slave, or the woman who touched Jesus' cloak, or Jairus who sought help for his daughter. Those came full of assurance and expectation, but this man comes with mixed feelings of hope and uncertainty, trust and reservations, faith and doubt, and that note is immediately picked up by Jesus: 'If you are able! – All things can be done for the one who believes.' A good answer, do you think? Well, yes and no, for while it states a truth most of us accept in theory, it also highlights the quandary we find ourselves in when it comes to putting faith into practice – a quandary perfectly summed up in the father's response. 'I believe,' he cries out immediately; 'help my unbelief!' (Mark 9:24).

How often have we echoed those words? They take us to the heart not just of this man's predicament but also of faith itself. On the surface, they seem to contradict themselves, the father, it would seem, needing to make up his mind where he stands. He does believe, yet he doesn't; he has faith, yet he hasn't – what kind of trust is that? Yet isn't this precisely how we often feel in all kinds of situations? We believe in our hearts, yet in our minds we're not quite so certain. We believe God can change people's lives but can he help in the mess we've made of ours? We believe he can transform even the worst of situations, but does that include the one we're in now? Somehow we can't quite suppress those niggling doubts and sneaking reservations that cause us to hold back, afraid of committing ourselves, reluctant to take the step of faith until our every question has been answered. Yet, of course, the father in this story took the step of faith despite his doubts; he came to Jesus and asked for help, and this was all Jesus required. Never mind that he wasn't sure, that questions still troubled him – he had been ready to come despite them all. Here, surely, is what faith is all about: not having the answers to every question, still less pretending we believe what we don't, but honestly offering to God the ounce of faith we have. If the father had allowed his doubts to win the day, he would have gone home with nothing changed, but he offered the faith he had, and it was enough.

The story of Peter in Matthew chapter 14 contains a similar message. The disciples have spent the night in a boat, tossed and turned in a storm, and suddenly, as morning breaks, they see a shadowy figure approaching them, a figure that appears somehow to be walking on the water! No wonder they cry out, 'It is a ghost!' – but then a familiar voice calls out to them, 'Take heart, it is I; do not be afraid' (Matthew 14:26-27, *NRSV*). Surely, it's Jesus; they'd recognise him anywhere . . . or would they? They're still not sure, so 'Peter answered him, "Lord, if it is you, command me to come to you on the water." He said, "Come." So Peter got out of the boat, started walking on the water, and came towards Jesus' (14:28-29, *NRSV*). It's a truly extraordinary demonstration of faith – or at least it is until he looks down and sees the water churning around him, and then, as fear takes hold, he begins to sink, crying out in panic. Faith once more turns to doubt; trust to anxiety as Peter is overwhelmed by the enormity of what he is doing, the impossibility of what he's taking on, and straightaway he begins to flounder. Yet, even then, there is faith in his doubt: 'Lord, save me!' He may not have trusted as much as he could and should have done, but it was still sufficient for him to call out, and immediately Jesus 'reached out his hand and caught him, saying, 'You of little faith, why did you doubt?' (Matthew 14:31).

Do you see the point here? In both the cases we've looked at, there have been questions of faith. 'Is it possible?' 'Can it be done?' 'How can it be?' All too easily those questions could have been the end of the story, but they weren't, because instead of dwelling on them Peter and the father of the epileptic boy were ready to take the leap of faith. The doubts were still there, just as real as before, but they responded and reached out to Jesus despite them. That's how we too must learn to live with our questions. We've observed that they can be of value in leading us to a greater under-standing of and maturity in faith. We've recognised that doubt can at times be a genuine expression of faith, something we only find the courage to face when our faith is strong enough to cope with it. We've acknowledged that our experience of life can raise issues that genuinely challenge our Christian convictions. All that is true, yet it is not the final word, for our faith does not depend on any collection of creeds, doctrinal statement or set of beliefs but on a personal experience of God in Christ made known through his Spirit. We come to know that God not through proving his existence or debating his nature but through responding to his love and committing ourselves to an ongoing relationship. Certainly we must face our questions honestly and openly, but not to the exclusion of all else. Sometimes we have to step out despite them, trusting that though we don't have the answers, God does. Instead of dwelling on *what* we don't know, we need to focus on *whom* we do, for what may seem impossible to us, defying all logic and reason, may be perfectly possible for him. To put it simply, as well as the faith *to* doubt we need faith *in* doubt, or, as the much-loved hymn of Charlotte Elliott puts it:

Just as I am, though tossed about,
with many a conflict, many a doubt,
fightings within and fears without,
O lamb of God, I come.

Summary

- Doubt and questions can be a bit like a 'Mile-a-minute Vine' – left unchecked, they rapidly take over, suffocating and strangling everything in their path. We need to find a way of controlling them before they control us.
- Two biblical incidents provide examples of the way we must temper doubt with faith. The father of the epileptic boy was willing to come to Jesus seeking help, even though he was unsure it was worth it. Part of him believed Jesus could do something, part didn't, but he was ready to take the leap of faith.
- Similarly, when he was called to walk to Jesus across the lake, Peter was ready to swallow his natural hesitation and respond. Even when he looked down and questions filled his mind as he saw the water swirling around him, he called out in faith.
- In each of these incidents we see faith within doubt. Peter and the father of the epileptic boy grappled with real questions but they did not allow these to stifle their trust and lead to paralysis.

- Though we may not have answers to all our questions, we know enough of Christ to put our trust in him and take the leap of faith. What we cannot do, he can. Despite our doubts, we need to focus finally on him.

Discussion

- Can you think of instances in daily life when we have to take something on faith, even though we may have many unanswered questions?
- Are there times when you had to take a leap of faith? What were they and what happened?
- Are there aspects of the gospel that you find hard to understand but that you are happy to take on trust? What are these?

Prayer

Lord,
    we want to believe,
    but at times we find it so hard.
There are too many things we cannot make sense of,
    that appear to contradict everything we are told about you,
    and on occasions, despite ourselves,
    there seem to be more questions than answers.
So now we bring you both our faith and our doubt,
    acknowledging each openly before you.
Take what we are
    and, by your grace, provide what we lack,
    so that our trust may grow
    and our faith be strengthened,
    until that day when we know and love you
    as much as you fully know and love us.
In your name we pray.
Amen.

Meditation of the father of the epileptic boy

Lord, I do believe,
    truly.
Despite my doubts,
    despite my questions,
    I do believe.
Not that my faith is perfect, I'm not saying that –
    there's still much that puzzles me,
    much I'd like to ask you about further, given half the chance.
But I believe you're different,
    that you can change lives in a way others can't;
    that you can bring hope where there's despair,
    joy where there's sorrow,
    peace where there's turmoil,
    and love where there's hate.
And I need those things now as never before,
    not for myself, but for my son.
He's suffering, you see,
    troubled in body and mind,
    day after day thrown into terrible convulsions.
And, Lord, I'm afraid of what might happen,
    what he might do to himself when the fits come upon him.
It's breaking my heart seeing him like this,
    having to stand by helpless as he writhes and groans.
Yet I've tried everything –
    every doctor,
    every healer,
    even your own disciples,
    all to no avail.
Not one has been able to help,
    none able to provide the answer I long to find.
So I've come finally to you,
    my last throw of the dice,
    and I'm begging you, Lord, help!
Oh I know I don't deserve it, I'm not pretending otherwise.

I have my doubts, all too many –
    barely understanding half of what you teach,
    and even what does make sense is hard to accept.
I've not got the makings of a disciple, I realise that –
    all kinds of things wrong in my life –
    ask anyone.
And though I want to change,
    to become the person you would have me be,
    I'm not sure I can come anywhere near it.
In fact, though I say I believe, I'm not even certain of that,
    for I'm torn in two,
    half of me sure, half of me not,
    my faith and doubt warring together,
    each battling for the upper hand,
    each ebbing and flowing as the mood takes me.
Yet I've seen what you've been able to do for others,
    I've heard about the wonders you perform,
    and I'm sure that if anyone can help me, then it's you.
So you see, I do believe a little,
    not as much as I'd like,
    not as much as I should,
    but I do believe,
    and I'm trying so hard to believe more.
In the meantime, I'm begging you, Lord,
    on bended knee, I'm begging you:
    help my unbelief.

Further reading: Luke 18:27

What is impossible for mortals is possible for God. (*NRSV*)

Suggestions for action

Instead of focusing on doubts and questions, take the leap of faith.

Closing prayer

Loving God,
    we offer you not just our faith
    but also our doubt,
    praying that you will use both to lead us closer to you.
Amen.

Sixth week

Beyond question

Opening prayer

From the cowardice that dare not face new truth,
  from the laziness that is content with half truth,
  from the arrogance that thinks it knows all truth,
Good Lord, deliver me.
Amen.

Kenyan prayer

Introduction

'There are more questions than answers' – so say the words of an old song, and many of us would concur with that assessment. It's true for many of us on a purely academic level – sit us down in front of an examination paper and the chances are we'd find several of the questions hard to answer – but, of course, questions sometimes go beyond observable fact and theory, as we saw in our last session. Is there any meaning to life? Why are we here? How do we make sense of evil and suffering? Add to these a host of moral and ethical questions, and it becomes plain just how difficult some things are to answer? Does this mean, then, that answers cannot be found, that we must simply hold up our hands and admit there are boundaries beyond which our knowledge cannot reach? Or should we still be always seeking to know and understand more, taking our comprehension of the universe to ever-greater heights? It is to this dichotomy that we turn in our final session. We do so not out of idle curiosity but because it raises important and potentially divisive issues concerning faith. Some will argue that we must hold firmly to revealed truth, irrespective of scientific research and discovery. If this means dismissing what others regard as indisputable, so be it. Others, conversely, maintain that we must abandon anything that cannot be squared with scientific method and our modern-day worldview, even if that means discarding previously accepted Christian doctrine. Is there a middle way between these two extremes, or must we decide between these stark choices?

Activity

Mastermind? (see page 83).

Reading: Psalm 131:1-3

My heart is not proud, O Lord, my eyes are not haughty; I do not concern myself with things too wonderful and awesome for me. But I have stilled and quieted my soul; like a weaned child with its mother, like a weaned child is my soul within me. Trust in the Lord, Israel, this day and always.

Comment

Do you remember the television series screened some years ago now called *Supersense*? It explored the special senses possessed by members of the animal kingdom, each offering a form of perception unlike anything we experience as human beings. Through skilled photography and visual effects, the programmes gave a fascinating insight into what these were, how they work and what they must feel like. On one level, the series elicited admiration at how much has been discovered through careful field observation and meticulous scientific research, opening up hitherto closed areas of knowledge. On another level, it brought home just how little we still know about the world and universe, for all the skill and ingenuity of humankind. Don't think I would downplay the advances that have been achieved. We understand the workings of the cosmos today better than at any time in human history, and we all benefit in innumerable ways from new discoveries being made each day. Admittedly, these bring with them moral and ethical dilemmas, sobering as well as exciting possibilities, and, at times, a challenge to our faith, but this should not and must not be used as an excuse for Christians adopting a head-in-the-sand mentality, retreating into an anti-intellectual ghetto resistant to questions of truth. At the same time, however, there *are* limitations to our understanding, and it is foolish to pretend otherwise. Just because we cannot grasp something doesn't mean it isn't true. It may be we need to learn more about it, or perhaps approach it from a different angle. It may be we are asking the wrong question, an apparent dilemma the result of us having our facts wrong. It may be that our minds are closed to certain possibilities, other people clearly able to see what our narrow horizons keep hidden from us. In other words, there comes a point when we must recognise our limitations and have the humility to admit that some truths are beyond us, some realities beyond our comprehension, part of a purpose greater than our own.

We see precisely such humility in Psalm 131, surely some of the loveliest words in the Old Testament. Here is the testimony of one whose mind is at peace after having been in turmoil, who has struggled with doubt and wrestled with questions only to tie himself into ever-increasing knots, but who has come back to the one sure thing he knows to be true: that God cares for him and watches over him as a mother cares for her child. What inspired these words of David we are not told. Perhaps they were written as he fled for his life from Saul, trying to make sense of why a man he had counted his friend was resolved to kill him. Perhaps they reflect his thoughts as he gazed at the vastness of the wilderness or night sky and marvelled at his own smallness against the immensity of it all. Perhaps they were written in a time of doubt, personal tragedy or crisis, forcing him to face difficult issues as never before.

Whatever it was, the result was a simple expression of faith and trust from one who clearly had wrestled with the mysteries of life and in the end had to concede defeat, leaving his questions in the hands of God.

Much the same conclusion is reached in the extraordinary story of Job, which we focused on in the second session. Of all people, you will recall, he had just cause to doubt, good reason to question, yet what answer did he finally receive? In one sense, it was no answer at all; in another, it is the answer to everything. 'Then the Lord answered Job out of the storm: "Who is this that speaks in the dark and questions me out of ignorance? Listen now – I will ask the questions and you can answer. Where were you when I established foundations for the earth? Tell me, if you know so much. Do you presume to put me in the wrong? Do you question my justice to justify yourself? Do you have an arm like God's arm, and can you thunder with a voice like his?"' (Job 38:1-2; 40:7; 38:4; 40:8-9). It's powerful stuff, isn't it, but do you get the point of what God is saying here? Job did. He recognised that God was putting him in his place, reminding him of the limitations of human knowledge. 'Then Job answered the Lord: "I know that you can do anything, and that nothing is beyond you. I have spoken of mysteries I do not understand, things so wonderful they are beyond my comprehension"' (42:1-2, 3b). After all his attempts to make sense of so much that apparently flew in the face of faith, Job had the faith and humility to confess he was dealing with mysteries beyond him. There were many ready to offer pat answers, including well-intentioned explanations in the context of faith, but he came to realise that when it comes to God there are some things that, in this life at least, we simply cannot understand. 'I am unworthy – what can I say? I shut my hand over my mouth. I spoke once, but I have no answer – twice, but I will say no more' (Job 40:4-5).

Accepting that we do not know. Is that a cop-out? Well, yes, if we're not very careful it can be precisely that. I've seen it used as such all too often, patent absurdities accepted in the name of faith and, by the same token, important questions ducked or side-stepped. That is the last thing I'd want to encourage. As we have observed several times in this course, life is full of mysteries and being a Christian doesn't mean we can avoid facing those. Childlike faith is not the same as childish faith, for God has consecrated our mind as well as our soul, our intellect as well as our heart. We cannot, then, approach every theological conundrum telling ourselves, 'Ah, but we're talking about God here', as though that presupposes an answer can never be found. Rather, we should search for enlightenment, strive for understanding, seek wisdom and guidance, and if we are still confronted by apparently irreconcilable paradox, *only then* should we appeal to the otherness of God, acknowledging that his ways are not always our ways or his thoughts our thoughts. Job's mistake was not in questioning, but in assuming he could find all the answers, and then challenging God's justice and concern when it turned out otherwise. He came to learn through painful experience that though some things defy understanding they are true nonetheless.

Some will still call this a cop-out, accusing me of a 'God-of-the-gaps' argument, justifying faith or avoiding complex issues through appealing to areas where human knowledge is incomplete. I can understand such a criticism, yet would contend that there is no way finally to avoid it. If God is who we say he is – the creator of the ends of the earth, ruler over space and time, before all, in all and beyond all – then inevitably there will come a point where we must acknowledge that our limited comprehension can go no further. In the end, having done our all, having searched honestly after truth and openly faced our questions, we must be willing to say with David, 'I do not concern myself with great matters or things too wonderful for me. But I have stilled and quieted my soul; like a weaned child with its mother, like a weaned child is my soul within me.' Or, as the Apostle Paul puts it in his letter to the Romans (11:33-36), 'O how great is the wealth of God's wisdom and knowledge; how unfathomable are his judgements and mysterious his ways. For who has known the Lord's mind, or who has been his counsellor, or who has given to him that they should be repaid? From him and to him and through him belong all things; to him be glory for all time. Amen.'

Summary

- There are other forms of perception besides the human senses. Although we have come to understand much about the mechanics of the universe, many things are still beyond human comprehension. Sometimes, we need to admit those limitations when it comes to making sense of the things of God.

- We see precisely this in the testimony of David in Psalm 131. Having wrestled with questions, he finally recognises the need to let go of them and to acknowledge the otherness of God.

- Similarly, Job reaches the point when he has to admit certain truths are beyond him. He has to acknowledge that we cannot always fathom the mind of God.

- This is not to suggest we shouldn't ask questions. It was precisely through doing so that Job and David came more fully to appreciate the wonder of God. Equally important, this brought home to them the inadequacy of many answers offered sincerely but tritely in the name of faith.

- Some may still feel that appealing to the otherness of God is a way of avoiding difficult issues and believing what we want to believe in the face of all reason. Should we refuse even to ask questions, this might be justified, but if God is who we believe he is, then there comes a point when accepting we do not and cannot come up with all the answers is inevitable.

- Alongside reason, there also has to be faith. Like Paul, we must eventually acknowledge in awe and wonder the unfathomable mystery of God.

Discussion

- Is your picture of God too small? Have you limited God to your own horizons, instead of allowing your horizons to be enlarged by God's greatness?

- Is appealing to the otherness of God a way of honestly tackling questions or simply an excuse to avoid facing them?

- Are there truths in life that can never be proven by reason? What are they? In what areas of faith do you feel we have to accept complete understanding is beyond us?

Prayer

Almighty and everlasting God,
  you are higher than our highest thoughts,
  but always close by our sides;
  greater than we can ever think or imagine,
  yet made known to us in Christ.
Though we stretch imagination to the limit,
  we barely begin to glimpse how wonderful you are.
Though you sometimes seem distant,
  always you are near.
Though life seems to make no sense,
  still you are present, your purpose unchanged.
Whatever we face,
  wherever we are,
  you are there,
  seen or unseen,
  your hand constantly at work.
Open our eyes afresh to your greatness,
  and remind us again that your ways are not *our* ways
  nor your thoughts *our* thoughts,
So may we glimpse once more your glory,
  and, though we do not always understand,
  may we walk in faith,
  in Jesus' name.
Amen.

Meditation of David

It's no good, Lord,
    it's too much for me,
    more than I can ever take in.
I've tried, you know that.
Day after day I've struggled
    to get my head round the wonder of who and what you are,
    but I just can't do it,
    your greatness beyond the reach of the human mind.
I've come far, no question,
    new insights and experiences adding to my sense of wonder,
    deepening my faith,
    enlarging my vision;
    yet I realise now that those were just a taste,
    a small sample of what is yet in store,
    for there is always more to learn,
    much that is hidden still to be revealed.
It's frightening, almost,
    for you overturn all our expectations,
    at work not just in the light but in the darkness,
    not just in the good but in the bad –
    no place outside your purpose
    no person beyond your grace,
    your love stronger, wider, greater, deeper
    than I've even begun to imagine!
Always you are there,
    one step ahead,
    waiting to take my hand
    and lead me on to the next stage of my journey.
So that's it, Lord;
    enough is enough –
    no more tying myself into knots,
    no more juggling with the impossible.
I don't have all the answers
    and I never will have,

but I've got you, here by my side,
behind to guard me,
ahead to lead me,
above to bless me,
within to feed me,
your love always there,
every moment,
everywhere,
in everything –
and, quite honestly, if I've got that, what else do I need to know!

Further reading: Isaiah 55:8-9; Psalm 139:1-2, 6

My thoughts are not your thoughts, nor are your ways my ways, says the Lord. For as the heavens are higher than the earth, so are my ways higher than your ways and my thoughts than your thoughts . . . O Lord, you have searched me and known me. You know when I sit down and when I rise up; you discern my thoughts from far away . . . Such knowledge is too wonderful for me; it is so high that I cannot attain it. (*NRSV*)

Suggestions for action

Instead of brooding over things you don't understand, swallow your pride and accept that some things are beyond you.

Closing prayer

Sovereign God,
    give us humility
    to acknowledge our weakness beside your greatness,
    faith to trust in you

despite our doubts and our blindness to your glory,
joy in knowing you,
despite the limitations of our understanding,
and peace in serving you,
knowing that you are the Lord of all, a God both near and far.
Through Jesus Christ our Lord.
Amen.

Appendix 1
Activities

First week: Learning through questions
What's my Line?

Play your own version of the old radio classic 'What's my Line?' (Select three members of the group to decide on the name of an unusual person or occupation which the remaining group members have to identify through asking up to twenty questions.) To make this more interesting and informative, find out if people in the group once had a job or career that none of the other participants knows of, and use these as your 'volunteers'.

Afterwards, talk about the importance of questions in learning, and discuss how far and in what ways we can relate this to faith.

Second week: Disturbing questions
Riddle

Allow sufficient time for everybody to work through the following riddle.

My first is in RIDDLE, HARD and INVOLVED,
My second's in QUESTION though also UNSOLVED,
My third is in PUZZLE, CONFOUND and CONFUSE,
My fourth is in TROUBLED as well as BEMUSE,
My last is in MYSTERY, TURMOIL and TEST.
The answer seems simple but not so the quest.

After everyone has found the answer, talk briefly together about the things that make life sometimes seem like a riddle. Ask how far these can lead to a crisis of faith, and whether members of the group have experienced such times.

Third week: The faith in question

Trivial Pursuit™

Read out a variety of questions from the board game Trivial Pursuit™. Play this as an open quiz rather than board game, or it will almost certainly take too long. Afterwards, discuss whether the questions were trivial, as the title of the game suggests. Ask what questions in life and faith we might justifiably describe as such; what destructive debates and arguments we might be drawn into as Christians that are ultimately peripheral to the gospel message.

Fourth week: Ultimate questions

The people in question

The quiz below concerns people who in a variety of ways have explored ultimate questions. Invite members of the group to identify those associated with each.

1. Who wrote *The Republic*?
2. Who said 'I think, therefore I am', or, more accurately, *'Je pense, donc je suis'*?
3. Which Syrian writer and painter wrote *The Prophet*?
4. Who penned the lines 'What is this life if, full of care, we have no time to stand and stare'?
5. Which French existentialist wrote the book *L'Etre et le néant* (Being and Nothingness) in 1943?
6. Which comedy team wrote and produced the spoof film *The Meaning of Life*?
7. We all know that Shakespeare wrote the words 'To be, or not to be, that is the question', but in which play are these words found, and what is the next line?
8. Who wrote *A Brief History of Time*, published in 1988 ?
9. Who wrote the book *Utopia*?
10. Which philosopher and theologian of the Middle Ages wrote

the *Summa theologiae*, an attempt, among other things, to prove the existence of God?

Fifth week: Living with questions

Pop-up Pirate™

If you are able to get hold of it, play a game or two of 'Pop-up Pirate', or one of the other similar games on the market (the aim of the game is to thrust plastic 'swords' into the miniature barrel without causing the pirate to leap up!). Afterwards, briefly discuss times when we have to take a leap of faith even though we are not sure we are doing the right thing. In what way is this similar to trusting in God despite having questions, and in what way is it different?

Alternatively, stage your own version of the TV show *Who wants to be a millionaire?* – even allowing 'Ask a friend' or 'Consult the audience' – and then talking afterwards about the leap of faith required in answering a question we are unsure of or in accepting the advice of others.

Sixth week: Beyond question

Mastermind?

The aim of this session is to bring home the limitations of our knowledge as individuals, and to stimulate discussion on whether some things will always deny the human intellect. In advance of the session, ask two people to help you in staging your own version of the quiz programme *Mastermind*. Ask one of them for their specialist subject, and then prepare 20 relatively easy questions on this. Tell the other person that their specialist subject is to be 'Anything and Everything'! For them, prepare 20 of the most obscure questions you can think of, making sure that you have a record of the answers. If possible, try to ensure that no one will know the answers to these. Stage your 'heat' of Mastermind, beginning with the participant whose specialist subject is genuine. Darken the room and fix up a lamp for effect, and allow two minutes for the participant to answer all the questions (they can, of course, pass if they do not know the answer). After each set of questions, give the answers to those answered incorrectly or where the participant passed. Afterwards, briefly discuss areas in which our knowledge is limited. Ask whether there are any truly unanswerable questions, and, if so, what these might be.

Appendix 2

Answers

Second week

The answer to the riddle is DOUBT.

Fourth week

1. Plato
2. René Descartes
3. Kahlil Gibran
4. W. H. Davies
5. Jean-Paul Sartre
6. Monty Python
7. *Hamlet*

   'To be, or not to be: that is the question:
   Whether 'tis nobler in the mind to suffer
   The slings and arrows of outrageous fortune,
   Or to take arms against a sea of troubles,
   And by opposing end them?'

8. Stephen Hawking
9. St Thomas More
10. St Thomas Aquinas

Also in this series:

Paul – the man and the mission
Something to share – communicating the good news
Prayer – the fundamental questions
Unsung gifts – the Spirit at work in the New Testament
Love – the key to it all
Discipleship – the journey of faith
Women of faith – what they teach us

Also by Nick Fawcett:

No ordinary man (books 1 and 2)
Resources for reflective worship on the person of Jesus

Grappling with God (books 1-4)
Old Testament studies for personal and small-group use

The unfolding story
Resources for reflective worship on the Old Testament

To put it another way
Resources for reflective worship on the Parables

Are you listening?
Honest prayers about life

Prayers for all seasons (books 1 and 2)
A comprehensive resource for public worship

Getting it across
One hundred talks for family worship

Decisions, decisions
A Lent study course

Promises, promises
An Advent study course

Daily prayer
A book of daily devotions

All the above titles are available from your local Christian bookshop or direct from Kevin Mayhew Ltd, telephone 01449 737978, fax: 01449 737834, email: sales@kevinmayhewltd.com